# ⸢Illustrated⸣

# CHRISTMAS ~ CAROLS

# [Illustrated]
# CHRISTMAS
# CAROLS

*Words and Music for over*
**40** *traditional songs*

*Arranged by Michael Haslam*
*Illustrated by Isabelle Brent*

Clarkson Potter/Publishers
New York

Published by Clarkson N. Potter, Inc., 201 East 50th Street,
New York, New York 10022. Member of the Crown Publishing Group.

Random House, Inc. New York, Toronto, London, Sydney, Auckland

First published in Great Britain by Ebury Press, an imprint of Random House UK Ltd.

CLARKSON N. POTTER, POTTER, and colophon are trademarks of Clarkson N. Potter, Inc.

Manufactured in Portugal

Design by Janet James
Picture research by Gabrielle Allen

Library of Congress Cataloging-in-Publication Data is available upon request.

ISBN 0-517-59547-8

10 9 8 7 6 5 4 3 2 1

First American Edition

# Contents

# Angels from the Realms of Glory

JAMES MONTGOMERY WROTE THE WORDS OF THIS JOYOUS
CAROL IN 1816 AND IT WAS FIRST PUBLISHED IN A NEWSPAPER
IN SHEFFIELD, ENGLAND, ON CHRISTMAS EVE.

1. Angels from the realms of glory,
    Wing your flight o'er all the earth;
Ye who sang creation's story
    Now proclaim Messiah's birth:

*Come and worship, come and worship,*
*Worship Christ the newborn King.*

2. Shepherds in the fields abiding,
    Watching o'er your flocks by night,
God with man is now residing;
    Yonder shines the infant Light:

3. Sages, leave your contemplations,
    Brighter visions beam afar;
Seek the great Desire of Nations,
    Ye have seen his natal star:

4. Saints before the altar bending,
    Watching long in hope and fear,
Suddenly the Lord, descending,
    In his temple shall appear:

5. Though an infant now we view him,
    He shall fill his Father's throne,
Gather all the nations to him;
    Every knee shall then bow down:

A merry Christmas

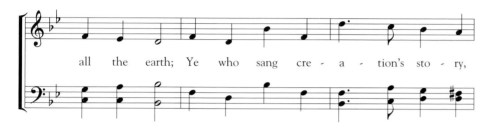

An - gels from the realms of glo - ry, Wing your flight o'er

all the earth; Ye who sang cre - a - tion's sto - ry,

Now pro - claim Mes - si - ah's birth: Come and wor - ship,

come and wor - ship, Wor - ship Christ the new - born King.

# As with Gladness Men of Old

W. Chatterton Dix wrote the words of this carol while recovering from a serious illness in 1858. The tune they fit so perfectly is an old German hymn tune.

1. As with gladness men of old
   Did the guiding star behold,
   As with joy they hailed its light,
   Leading onward, beaming bright,
   So, most gracious God, may we
   Evermore be led to thee.

2. As with joyful steps they sped,
   To that lowly manger-bed,
   There to bend the knee before
   Him whom heaven and earth adore,
   So may we with willing feet
   Ever seek thy mercy-seat.

3. As they offered gifts most rare
   At that manger rude and bare,
   So may we with holy joy,
   Pure, and free from sin's alloy,
   All our costliest treasures bring,
   Christ, to thee our heavenly King.

4. Holy Jesu, every day
   Keep us in the narrow way;
   And, when earthly things are past,
   Bring our ransomed souls at last
   Where they need no star to guide,
   Where no clouds thy glory hide.

5. In the heavenly country bright
   Need they no created light;
   Thou its Light, its Joy, its Crown,
   Thou its Sun which goes not down:
   There for ever may we sing
   Alleluyas to our King.

A JOLLY CHRISTMAS MAY YOURS BE

Pain Bros Wholesale Art Traders Hastings          Printed in Berlin

As with gladness men of old Did the guiding

star be-hold, As with joy they hailed its light,

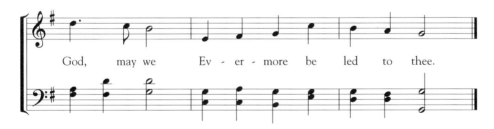

Lead-ing on-ward, beam-ing bright, So, most gra-cious

God, may we Ev-er-more be led to thee.

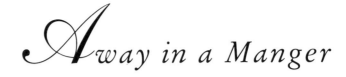

# Away in a Manger

THE TUNE FOR THIS LOVELY CHILDREN'S CAROL WAS WRITTEN IN PHILADELPHIA BY WILLIAM KIRKPATRICK IN 1885. IT IS NOT KNOWN WHO WROTE THE WORDS.

1. Away in a manger, no crib for a bed,
   The little Lord Jesus laid down his sweet head,
   The stars in the bright sky looked down where he lay,
   The little Lord Jesus asleep on the hay.

2. The cattle are lowing, the baby awakes,
   But little Lord Jesus no crying he makes.
   I love thee, Lord Jesus! Look down from the sky,
   And stay by my side until morning is nigh.

3. Be near me, Lord Jesus; I ask Thee to stay
   Close by me for ever, and love me, I pray.
   Bless all the dear children in thy tender care,
   And fit us for heaven, to live with thee there.

Ring the joybells - ring!
Christ is born - our King!

A - way in a\_\_ man - ger, no\_\_ crib for a bed, The\_\_

lit - tle Lord Je - sus laid\_\_ down his sweet head. The

stars in the\_\_ bright sky looked\_\_ down where he lay. The\_\_

lit - tle Lord Je - sus a - sleep on the hay.

# Brightest and Best of the Sons of the Morning

THIS CAROL BY A YOUNG MAN WHO LATER BECAME A BISHOP
CELEBRATES THE EPIPHANY OR THE COMING OF THE WISE MEN.
EPIPHANY IS CELEBRATED BY THE CHURCH ON JANUARY 6.

1.  Brightest and best of the sons of the morning,
        Dawn on our darkness and lend us thine aid;
    Star of the East, the horizon adorning,
        Guide where our infant Redeemer is laid.

2.  Cold on his cradle the dew-drops are shining,
        Low lies his head with the beasts of the stall:
    Angels adore him in slumber reclining,
        Maker and Monarch and Saviour of all.

3.  Say, shall we yield him, in costly devotion,
        Odours of Edom and offerings divine?
    Gems of the mountain and pearls of the ocean,
        Myrrh from the forest or gold from the mine?

4.  Vainly we offer each ample oblation,
        Vainly with gifts would his favour secure;
    Richer by far is the heart's adoration,
        Dearer to God are the prayers of the poor.

5.  Brightest and best of the sons of the morning,
        Dawn on our darkness and lend us thine aid;
    Star of the East, the horizon adorning,
        Guide where our infant Redeemer is laid.

Bright - est and best of the sons of the morn - ing

Dawn on our dark - ness and lend us thine aid;

Star of the East, the ho - ri - zon a - dor - ning,

Guide where our in - fant Re - deem - er is laid.

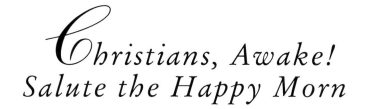

# Christians, Awake!
## Salute the Happy Morn

JOHN BYROM WROTE THE WORDS OF THIS CAROL AND GAVE THEM
TO HIS DAUGHTER AS A CHRISTMAS PRESENT. A LOCAL MUSICIAN
WROTE THE TUNE ON THE SAME DAY AND SENT A CHOIR TO SING
THE COMPLETE CAROL UNDER MR BYROM'S WINDOW.

1.   Christians, awake! Salute the happy morn,
Whereon the Saviour of the world was born;
Rise to adore the mystery of love,
Which hosts of Angels chanted from above;
With them the joyful tidings first begun
Of God incarnate and the Virgin's Son:

2.   Then to the watchful shepherds it was told,
Who heard the angelic herald's voice, "Behold,
I bring good tidings of a Saviour's birth
To you and all the nations upon earth;
This day hath God fulfilled his promised word,
This day is born a Saviour, Christ the Lord."

*continued overleaf*

Christ - ians, a - wake! Sa - lute the hap - py morn, Where - on the

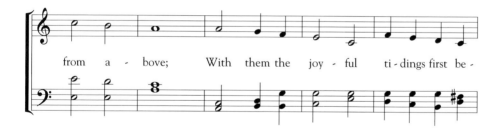

Sa - viour of the world was born; Rise to a - dore the

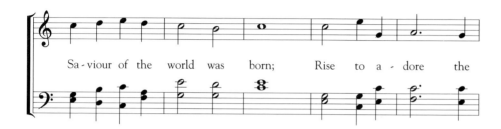

my - ste - ry of love, Which hosts of an - gels chant - ed

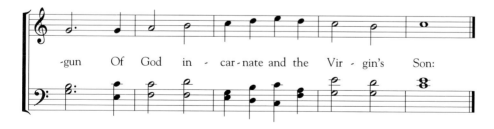

from a - bove; With them the joy - ful ti - dings first be -

-gun Of God in - car - nate and the Vir - gin's Son:

3. He spake; and straightway the celestial choir
   In hymns of joy, unknown before, conspire.
   The praises of redeeming love they sang,
   And heaven's whole orb with Alleluyas rang:
   God's highest glory was their anthem still,
   Peace upon earth, and mutual goodwill.

4. To Bethlehem straight the enlightened shepherds ran,
   To see the wonder God had wrought for man,
   And found, with Joseph and the blessed Maid,
   Her Son, the Saviour, in a manger laid;
   Amazed the wondrous story they proclaim,
   The first apostles of his infant fame.

5. Like Mary let us ponder in our mind
   God's wondrous love in saving lost mankind;
   Trace we the Babe, who hath retrieved our loss,
   From his poor manger to his bitter cross;
   Then may we hope, angelic thrones among,
   To sing, redeemed, a glad triumphal song.

God Jul

Christ - ians, a - wake! Sa - lute the hap - py morn, Where - on the

Sa - viour of the world was born; Rise to a - dore the

my - ste - ry of love, Which hosts of an - gels chant - ed

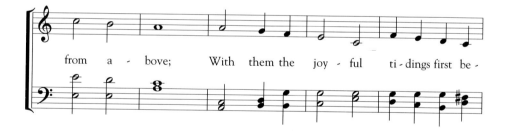

from a - bove; With them the joy - ful ti - dings first be -

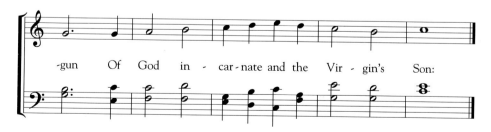

-gun Of God in - car - nate and the Vir - gin's Son:

# Coventry Carol

THIS OLD CAROL HAS A STRANGE,
SAD QUALITY AND CAN BE SUNG SLOWLY.

---

*Lully, lulla, thou little, tiny child; By, by, lully, lullay.*

1. O sisters too,
   How may we do
       For to preserve this day
   This poor youngling
   For whom we do sing
       "By, by, lully, lullay"?

2. Herod the King
   In his raging
       Chargèd he hath this day
   His men of might,
   In his own sight
       All young children to slay.

3. That woe is me,
   Poor child, for thee,
       And ever mourn and say:
   For thy parting
   Neither say nor sing
       "By, by, lully, lullay".

*Lully, lulla, thou little, tiny child; By, by, lully, lullay.*

Lul - ly, lul - la, thou lit - tle ti - ny child, By by, lul -

-ly lul - lay.      O sis - ters too,   How   may   we   do

For   to   pre - serve this      day   This   poor   young - ling   for

whom   we   do   sing      "By   by,   lul - ly   lul - lay"?

Repeat Refrain only after verse 3

# *Deck the Hall with Boughs of Holly*

THIS BOISTEROUS CAROL IS FROM WALES AND WAS
ORIGINALLY SUNG ON NEW YEAR'S EVE.

———

1. Deck the hall with boughs of holly,
   *Fa la la la la la la la lah.*
   'Tis the season to be jolly,
   *Fa la la la la la la la lah.*
   Fill the mead cup, drain the barrel,
   *Fa la la la la la, la la lah.*
   Troll the ancient Christmas carol,
   *Fa la la la la la la la lah.*

2. See the flowing bowl before us,
   *Fa la la la la la la la lah.*
   Strike the harp and join the chorus,
   *Fa la la la la la la la lah.*
   Follow me in merry measure,
   *Fa la la la la la, la la lah.*
   While I sing of beauty's treasure,
   *Fa la la la la la la la lah.*

3. Fast away the old year passes,
   *Fa la la la la la la la lah.*
   Hail the new, ye lads and lassies,
   *Fa la la la la la la la lah.*
   Laughing, quaffing, all together,
   *Fa la la la la la, la la lah.*
   Heedless of the wind and weather,
   *Fa la la la la la la la lah.*

# Ding, dong! Merrily on High

THE WORDS ARE BY G.R. WOODWARD, WHILE THE TUNE IS
FRENCH AND DATES FROM THE SIXTEENTH CENTURY. *IO* IN
VERSE TWO MEANS 'JOY' AND IS PRONOUNCED *EE-OH*.

1.  Ding, dong! Merrily on high
        In heav'n the bells are ringing:
    Ding, dong! Verily the sky
        Is riv'n with angels singing.

    *Gloria, Hosanna in excelsis!*

2.  E'en so here below, below,
        Let steeple bells be swungen,
    And *io, io, io,*
        By priest and people sungen.

3.  Pray you, dutifully prime
        Your matin chime, ye ringers;
    May you beautifully rime
        Your evetime song, ye singers.

Ding, dong! Mer - ri - ly on high   In   heav'n the bells are   ring - ing:

Ding, dong! Ve - ri - ly the sky   Is   riv'n with An - gels   sing - ing.

Glo - - - - - - -

- - - - - ri - a, Ho - san - na in ex - cel - sis!

Ring the joybells - ring!
Christ is born - our King!

# 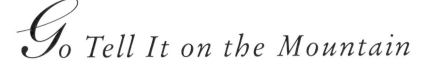Go Tell It on the Mountain

THIS AMERICAN CAROL IS A TRADITIONAL SPIRITUAL. THERE IS
A GREAT CONTRAST BETWEEN THE VERSE AND THE LIVELY CHORUS.

1. When I was a seeker
    I sought both night and day,
I asked the Lord to help me,
    And He showed me the way.

*Go tell it on the mountain,*
    *Over the hills and everywhere,*
*Go tell it on the mountain,*
    *Our Jesus Christ is born.*

2. He made me a watchman
    Upon a city wall,
And if I am a Christian,
    I am the least of all.

When I was a seek - er I sought both night and day, I

asked the Lord to help me, and he showed me the way.

Go tell it on the moun - tain, O - ver the hills and ev' - ry - where,

Go tell it on the moun - tain, Our Je - sus Christ is born.

# God Rest you Merry, Gentlemen

'LET GOD KEEP YOU MERRY' IS WHAT THE OPENING WORDS MEAN.
IN THE FOURTH VERSE THE FAMILIAR 'FRIENDS' OF SATAN
WERE PROBABLY THE 'FIENDS' OF SATAN ORIGINALLY.

---

1. God rest you merry, gentlemen, let nothing you dismay,
   For Jesus Christ our Saviour was born upon this day,
   To save us all from Satan's power when we were gone astray:

   *O tidings of comfort and joy, comfort and joy,*
   *O tidings of comfort and joy.*

2. In Bethlehem in Jewry this blessed babe was born,
   And laid within a manger upon this blessed morn;
   The which His mother Mary nothing did take in scorn;

3. From God our heavenly Father a blessed Angel came,
   And unto certain shepherds brought tidings of the same,
   How that in Bethlehem was born the Son of God by name:

*continued overleaf*

26

God rest you mer-ry, gen-tle-men, let no-thing you dis-may, For
Je-sus Christ our Sa-viour was born up-on this day, To
save us all from Sa-tan's power when we were gone a-stray: O-
ti-dings of com-fort and joy, com-fort and joy, O-
ti-dings of com-fort and joy.

27

4. "Fear not," then said the Angel, "Let nothing you afright,
   This day is born a Saviour of virtue, power, and might;
   So frequently to vanquish all the friends of Satan quite":

5. The shepherds at those tidings rejoicèd much in mind,
   And left their flocks a-feeding in tempest, storm and wind,
   And went to Bethlehem straightway this blessed babe to find:

6. But when to Bethlehem they came, whereat this infant lay,
   They found Him in a manger where oxen feed on hay,
   His mother Mary kneeling unto the Lord did pray:

7. Now to the Lord sing praises, all you within this place,
   And with true love and brotherhood each other now embrace;
   This holy tide of Christmas all others doth deface:

God rest you mer - ry, gen - tle - men, let no - thing you dis - may, For

Je - sus Christ our Sa - viour was born up - on this day, To

save us all from Sa - tan's power when we were gone a - stray: O -

ti - dings of com - fort and joy, com - fort and joy, O

ti - dings of com - fort and joy. _____

# Good King Wenceslas

ALTHOUGH JOHN MCNEALE INVENTED THE STORY TOLD IN THIS
CAROL, IT IS ONE OF THE FEW CAROLS WHERE ALL THE VERSES
ARE AS MEMORABLE AS THE FIRST.

1. Good King Wenceslas looked out
   On the feast of Stephen,
   When the snow lay round about,
   Deep and crisp and even:
   Brightly shone the moon that night,
   Though the frost was cruel,
   When a poor man came in sight
   Gathering winter fuel.

2. "Hither, page, and stand by me,
   If thou know'st it, telling,
   Yonder peasant, who is he?
   Where and what his dwelling?"
   "Sire, he lives a good league hence,
   Underneath the mountain,
   Right against the forest fence,
   By Saint Agnes' fountain."

3. "Bring me flesh, and bring me wine,
   Bring me pine-logs hither:
   Thou and I will see him dine,
   When we bear them thither."
   Page and monarch, forth they went,
   Forth they went together;
   Through the rude wind's wild lament
   And the bitter weather.

4. "Sire, the night is darker now,
   And the wind blows stronger;
   Fails my heart, I know not how;
   I can go no longer."
   "Mark my footsteps, good my page;
   Tread thou in them boldly;
   Thou shalt find the winter's rage
   Freeze thy blood less coldly."

5. In his master's steps he trod,
   Where the snow lay dinted;
   Heat was in the very sod
   Which the Saint had printed.
   Therefore, Christian men, be sure,
   Wealth or rank possessing,
   Ye who now will bless the poor,
   Shall yourselves find blessing.

Good King Wen - ces - las looked out   On the feast of   Ste - phen,

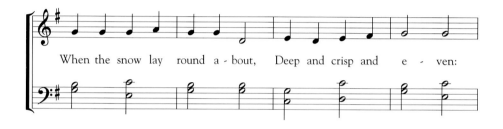

When the snow lay round a - bout,   Deep and crisp and   e - ven:

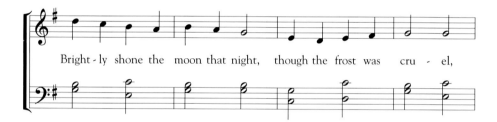

Bright - ly shone the moon that night,   though the frost was   cru - el,

When a poor man came in sight Gath' - ring win - ter   fu - el.

# Green Grow'th the Holly

THIS OLD CAROL MAY HAVE BEEN WRITTEN BY KING HENRY VIII.
ADDITIONAL WORDS HAVE BEEN ADDED MORE RECENTLY BY
LADY MARY TREFUSIS.

1. Green grow'th the holly, so doth the ivy;
   Though winter blasts blow ne'er so high,
   Green grow'th the holly.

2. Bright are the flowers, hedgerows and ploughlands;
   The days grow longer in the sun,
   Soft fall the showers.

3. Full gold the harvest, grain for thy labour;
   With God must work for daily bread,
   Else, man, thou starvest.

4. Fast fall the shed leaves, russet and yellow;
   But resting-buds are snug and safe
   Where swung the dead leaves.

5. Green grow'th the holly, so doth the ivy;
   The God of life can never die.
   Green grow'th the holly.

A GLAD CHRISTMAS.

Green grow'th the hol - ly, so doth the i - vy; Though

win - ter blasts blow ne'er_____ so

high, Green grow'th the hol - ly.

# Hark! the Herald Angels Sing

THREE WRITERS CONTRIBUTED TO THE FINAL VERSION OF THE
ORIGINAL HYMN BY CHARLES WESLEY, THE FOUNDER OF
METHODISM. THE TUNE IS BY MENDELSSOHN.

———————

1. Hark! the herald Angels sing:
   "Glory to the newborn King!
   Peace on earth, and mercy mild,
   God and sinners reconciled."
   Joyful, all ye nations, rise,
   Join the triumph of the skies;
   With the angelic host proclaim,
   "Christ is born in Bethlehem."

   *Hark! the herald Angels sing,*
   *"Glory to the newborn King!"*

2. Christ, by highest heav'n adored:
   Christ the everlasting Lord;
   Late in time behold him come,
   Offspring of a Virgin's womb.
   Veil'd in flesh, the Godhead see:
   Hail, the incarnate Deity:
   Pleased as man with man to dwell,
   Jesus our Emmanuel!

3. Hail! the heaven-born Prince of peace!
   Hail! the Son of Righteousness!
   Light and life to all he brings,
   Risen with healing in his wings;
   Mild he lays his glory by,
   Born that man no more may die:
   Born to raise the sons of earth,
   Born to give them second birth.

Hark! the her - ald An - gels sing:___ "Glo - ry to the new-born King!

Peace on earth, and mer - cy mild,___ God and sin - ners re - con - ciled."

Joy - ful, all ye na - tions rise,___ Join the tri - umph of the skies;___

With th'an - ge - lic host pro - claim "Christ is___born in Beth - le - hem."

*Hark the her - ald An - gels sing,* "Glo - ry___to the new - born King!"

# I Heard the Bells on Christmas Day

HENRY WADSWORTH LONGFELLOW WROTE THIS VERY PERSONAL
EXPRESSION OF FAITH AND HOPE IN THE PREVAILING OF RIGHT OVER
WRONG.

1. I heard the bells on Christmas day
    Their old familiar carols play
        And mild and sweet the words repeat,
    Of peace on earth, good will to men.

2. I thought how as the day had come,
    The belfries of all Christendom
        Had rolled along th'unbroken song
    Of peace on earth, good will to men.

3. And in despair I bowed my head:
    "There is no peace on earth," I said,
        "For hate is strong, and mocks the song
    Of peace on earth, good will to men."

4. Then pealed the bells more loud and deep:
    "God is not dead, nor doth He sleep;
        The wrong shall fail, the right prevail,
    With peace on earth, good will to men."

5. 'Till, ringing, singing on its way,
    The world revolved from night to day,
        A voice, a chime, a chant sublime,
    Of peace on earth, good will to men!

I heard the bells on Christ - mas Day Their
old fa - mi - liar ca - rols play And mild and sweet the
words re - peat, Of peace on earth, good - will to men.

# I Saw Three Ships

THIS POPULAR FOLK-SONG CAROL WAS SUNG THROUGHOUT
ENGLAND AND DIFFERENT VERSIONS OF IT WERE PUBLISHED IN
THE EIGHTEENTH-CENTURY SINGLE-SHEET BROADSHEETS.

———————

1. I saw three ships come sailing in,
    *On Christmas Day, on Christmas Day,*
  I saw three ships come sailing in,
    *On Christmas Day in the Morning.*

2. And what was in those ships all three?

3. Our Saviour Christ and his lady.

4. Pray, whither sailed those ships all three?

5. O, they sailed into Bethlehem.

6. And all the bells on earth shall ring,

7. And all the Angels in heaven shall sing,

8. And all the souls on earth shall sing,

9. Then let us all rejoice amain!

I saw three ships come sail - ing in, On

Christ - mas Day, on Christ - mas Day, I saw three ships come

sail - ing in, On Christ - mas Day in the morn - ing.

# In Dulci Jubilo

THE MUSIC OF THIS GERMAN CAROL DATES FROM THE
FOURTEENTH CENTURY AND THE WORDS WERE FIRST PUT
INTO ENGLISH IN 1540. FOUR YEARS AFTER THE FOUNDING
OF PENNSYLVANIA, ITS CITIZENS SANG THIS CAROL IN
THIRTEEN LANGUAGES SIMULTANEOUSLY!

1. *In dulci jubilo*
   Now sing with hearts a-glow!
      Our delight and pleasure
   Lies *in praesepio*,
      Like sunshine is our treasure
   *Matris in gremio*
   *Alpha es et O!*
   *Alpha es et O!*

2. *O Jesu, parvule,*
   For thee I long alway;
      Comfort my heart's blindness,
   *O puer optime,*
      With all thy loving-kindness,
   *O princeps gloriae*
   *Trahe me post te!*
   *Trahe me post te!*

3. *O Patris caritas!*
   *O Nati lenitas!*
      Deeply were we stainèd
   *Per nostra crimina;*
      But thou for us hast gainèd
   *Coelorum gaudia,*
   O that we were there!
   O that we were there!

4. *Ubi sunt gaudia*
   In any place but there?
      There are angels singing
   *Nova cantica,*
      And there the bells are ringing
   *In Regis curia,*
   O that we were there!
   O that we were there!

In dul - ci ju - bi - lo _____ Now sing with

hearts a - glow! _____ Our de - light and plea - sure Lies

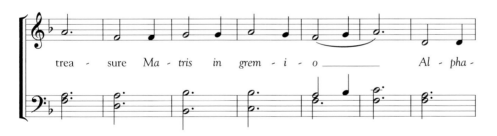

in prae - se - pi - o, _____ Like sun - shine is our

trea - sure Ma - tris in grem - i - o _____ Al - pha

es - et O! _____ Al - pha es et O! _____

# In the Bleak Mid-winter

THE TUNE IS BY GUSTAV HOLST, THE COMPOSER OF
*THE PLANETS*. THE WORDS ARE IRREGULAR SO YOU
HAVE TO ADAPT THE TUNE FOR LATER VERSES.

————————

1. In the bleak mid-winter
        Frosty wind made moan,
   Earth stood hard as iron,
        Water like a stone;
   Snow had fallen, snow on snow,
        Snow on snow,
   In the bleak mid-winter,
        Long ago.

2. Our God, heav'n cannot hold Him
        Nor earth sustain;
   Heav'n and earth shall flee away
        When He comes to reign;
   In the bleak mid-winter
        A stable place sufficed
   The Lord God Almighty
        Jesus Christ.

3. Enough for Him, whom Cherubim
        Worship night and day,
   A breastful of milk,
        And a mangerful of hay;
   Enough for Him, whom Angels
        Fall down before,
   The ox and ass and camel
        Which adore.

4. Angels and Archangels
        May have gathered there,
   Cherubim and Seraphim
        Thronged the air—
   But only His mother
        In her maiden bliss
   Worshipped the Beloved
        With a kiss.

5. What can I give Him
        Poor as I am?
   If I were a shepherd
        I would bring a lamb;
   If I were a wise man
        I would do my part;
   Yet what can I give Him—
        Give my heart.

In the bleak mid - win - ter    Frost - y wind made moan,

Earth stood hard as i - ron,    Wa - ter like a stone;

Snow had fal - len, snow on snow,    Snow____ on____ snow,

In  the bleak mid - win - ter,    Long___ a - go.

# *It Came Upon the Midnight Clear*

EDMUND SEARS WROTE THE WORDS IN WAYLAND,
MASSACHUSETTS AND THE TUNE IS BY
RICHARD S. WILLIS.

1. It came upon the midnight clear,
    That glorious song of old,
   From Angels bending near the earth
    To touch their harps of gold:
   "Peace on the earth, goodwill to men,
    From heaven's all-gracious King!"
   The world in solemn stillness lay
    To hear the Angels sing.

2. Still through the cloven skies they
    come,
    With peaceful wings unfurled;
   And still their heavenly music floats
    O'er all the weary world;
   Above its sad and lowly plains
    They bend on hovering wing;
   And ever o'er its Babel sounds
    The blessed Angels sing.

3. Yet with the woes of sin and strife
    The world has suffered long;
   Beneath the Angel-strain have rolled
    Two thousand years of wrong;
   And man, at war with man, hears not
    The love-song which they bring:
   O hush the noise, ye men of strife,
    And hear the Angels sing!

4. And ye, beneath life's crushing load,
    Whose forms are bending low,
   Who toil along the climbing way
    With painful steps and slow,
   Look now! for glad and golden hours
    Come swiftly on the wing;
   O rest beside the weary road,
    And hear the Angels sing!

5. For lo! the days are hastening on,
    By prophet-bards foretold,
   When, with the ever-circling years,
    Comes round the age of gold;
   When peace shall over all the earth
   Its ancient splendours fling,
    And the whole world send back the song
   Which now the Angels sing.

44

It came up-on the mid-night clear, That glo-rious song___ of

old,_____ From An-gels bend - ing near the earth To

touch their harps of gold:_____ "Peace on the earth,_ good-

will to men, From heav'n's_ all gra - cious King!"_____ The

world in so - lemn still - ness lay to hear the An - gels sing.___

# Jingle Bells

THIS SLEIGHING SONG IS BY JAMES PIERPOINT AND IS
PARTICULARLY POPULAR WITH CHILDREN.

1. Dashing through the snow
     On a one-horse open sleigh,
   O'er the fields we go,
     Laughing all the way.
   Bells on bob-tail ring,
     Making spirits bright;
   Oh, what fun it is to sing
     A sleighing song tonight.

   *Jingle Bells, Jingle Bells, Jingle all the way,*
   *Oh, what fun it is to ride on a one-horse open sleigh!*
   *Jingle Bells, Jingle Bells, Jingle all the way,*
   *Oh, what fun it is to ride on a one-horse open sleigh!*

2. Now the ground is white
     Go it while you're young.
   Let us take a ride
     And sing this sleighing song.
   Just get a bob-tail bay,
     Two-forty for his speed,
   Then hitch him to an open sleigh
     And crack! you'll take the lead.

# Joy to the World!

THIS IS ONE OF THE BEST OF THE THOUSANDS OF HYMNS
PENNED BY ISAAC WATTS. THE TUNE IS BY THE COMPOSER OF
*MESSIAH* – GEORGE FREDERICK HANDEL.

---

1. Joy to the world! the Lord is come;
    Let earth receive her King;
  Let every heart prepare him room,
    And heav'n and nature sing,
    And heav'n and nature sing,
    And heav'n, and heav'n and nature sing.

2. Joy to the world! the Saviour reigns:
    Let men their songs employ,
  While fields and floods, rocks, hills and plains,
    Repeat the sounding joy,
    Repeat the sounding joy,
    Repeat, repeat the sounding joy.

3. No more let sins and sorrows grow,
    Nor thorns infest the ground;
  He comes to make his blessings flow
    Far as the curse is found,
    Far as the curse is found,
    Far as, far as the curse is found.

4. He rules the world with truth and grace,
    And makes the nations prove
  The glories of his righteousness,
    And wonders of his love,
    And wonders of his love,
    And wonders, wonders of his love.

A merry Christmas

Joy to the world! the Lord is come; Let earth re - ceive her

King; Let ev' - ry heart____ pre - pare____ him____ room,____ And

heav'n and na - ture__ sing, And__ heav'n and na - ture__ sing, And__

heav'n, and heav'n____ and na - ture sing.

# O Christmas Tree

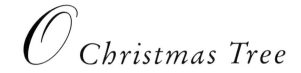

IN 1824 ERNST ANSCHÜTZ WROTE THE GERMAN WORDS
TO THIS CAROL WHICH IS CALLED *O TANNENBAUM*
IN THE ORIGINAL. THE TUNE IS ALSO SUNG TO THE
WORDS OF THE *RED FLAG*.

———————

1.  O Christmas tree, O Christmas tree!
       Thou tree most fair and lovely!
    O Christmas tree, O Christmas tree!
       Thou tree most fair and lovely!
    The sight of thee at Christmastide
       Spreads hope and gladness far and wide.
    O Christmas tree, O Christmas tree!
       Thou tree most fair and lovely!

2.  O Christmas tree, O Christmas tree!
       Thou hast a wondrous message.
    O Christmas tree, O Christmas tree!
       Thou hast a wondrous message.
    Thou dost proclaim the Saviour's birth,
       Goodwill to men and peace on earth.
    O Christmas tree, O Christmas tree!
       Thou hast a wondrous message.

O Christ - mas tree, O Christ - mas tree! Thou tree most fair and

love - ly! O Christ - mas tree, O Christ - mas tree! Thou

tree most fair and love - ly! The sight of thee at

Christ - mas - tide Spreads hope and glad - ness far and wide. O

Christ - mas tree, O Christ - mas tree! Thou tree most fair and love - ly!

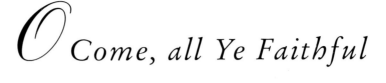

# O Come, all Ye Faithful

THE LAST VERSE OF THIS POPULAR HYMN IS TRADITIONALLY
SUNG ONLY ON CHRISTMAS EVE AND CHRISTMAS DAY.

1. O come, all ye faithful,
   Joyful and triumphant,
   O come ye, O come ye to Bethlehem;
   Come and behold him,
   Born the King of Angels:

   *O come let us adore him,*
   *O come let us adore him,*
   *O come let us adore him, Christ the Lord.*

2. God of God,
   Light of Light,
   Lo, he abhors not the Virgin's womb;
   Very God,
   Begotten not created:

3. Sing, choirs of angels,
   Sing in exultation,
   Sing, all ye citizens of heav'n above;
   Glory to God
   In the highest:

4. Yea, Lord, we greet thee,
   Born this happy morning,
   Jesu, to thee be glory given;
   Word of the Father,
   Now in flesh appearing:

Ring the joybells – ring!
Christ is born – our King!

O come, all ye faith - ful, Joy - ful and tri - um - phant, O

come ye, O come__ ye to Beth - le - hem;

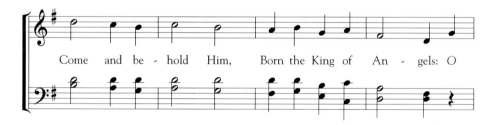

Come and be - hold Him, Born the King of An - gels: O

come, let us a - dore Him, O come let us a - dore Him, O

come let us a - dore Him,__ Christ ____ the Lord.

# O Come, O Come, Emmanuel!

THIS GREAT ADVENT HYMN CELEBRATES THE COMING OF JESUS
INTO THE WORLD FOR OUR SALVATION.
*EMMANUEL* MEANS 'GOD WITH US'.

1. O come, O come, Emmanuel!
   Redeem thy captive Israel,
       That into exile drear is gone
       Far from the face of God's dear Son.

   *Rejoice! Rejoice!*
   *Emmanuel shall come to thee, O Israel.*

2. O come, thou Branch of Jesse! Draw
   The quarry from the lion's claw;
       From the dread caverns of the grave,
       From nether hell, thy people save.

3. O come, O come, thou Dayspring bright!
   Pour on our souls thy healing light;
       Dispel the long night's lingering gloom,
       And pierce the shadows of the tomb.

4. O come, thou Lord of David's Key!
   The royal door fling wide and free;
       Safeguard for us the heav'nward road,
       And bar the way to death's abode.

5. O come, O come, Adonai,
   Who in thy glorious majesty
       From that high mountain clothed with awe
       Gavest thy folk the elder law.

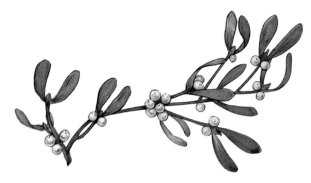

# O Little Town of Bethlehem

BISHOP PHILLIPS BROOKS, FROM PHILADELPHIA,
WROTE THIS CAROL FOR HIS SUNDAY SCHOOL IN 1868,
INSPIRED BY A PILGRIMAGE HE HAD MADE TO BETHLEHEM.
THE TUNE IS BY LEWIS H. REDNER.

1. O little town of Bethlehem,
   How still we see thee lie!
   Above thy deep and dreamless sleep
   The silent stars go by.
   Yet in thy dark streets shineth
   The everlasting light;
   The hopes and fears of all the years
   Are met in thee tonight.

2. O morning stars, together
   Proclaim the holy birth,
   And praises sing to God the King,
   And peace to men on earth;
   For Christ is born of Mary;
   And, gathered all above,
   While mortals sleep, the Angels keep
   Their watch of wondering love.

3. How silently, how silently,
   The wondrous gift is given!
   So God imparts to human hearts
   The blessings of his heaven.
   No ear may hear his coming;
   But in this world of sin,
   Where meek souls will receive him, still
   The dear Christ enters in.

4. Where children pure and happy
   Pray to the blessed Child,
   Where misery cries out to thee,
   Son of the mother mild;
   Where charity stands watching
   And faith holds wide the door,
   The dark night wakes, the glory breaks,
   And Christmas comes once more.

5. O holy Child of Bethlehem,
   Descend to us, we pray;
   Cast out our sin, and enter in,
   Be born in us today.
   We hear the Christmas Angels
   The great glad tidings tell:
   O Come to us, abide with us,
   Our Lord Emmanuel.

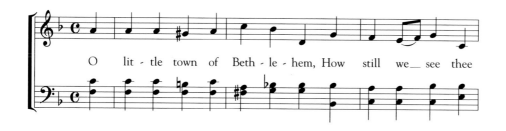

O lit - tle town of Beth - le - hem, How still we__ see thee

lie! A - bove thy deep and dream - less sleep The

si - lent__ stars go by. Yet in thy dark streets

shi - neth The e - ver - last - ing light; The

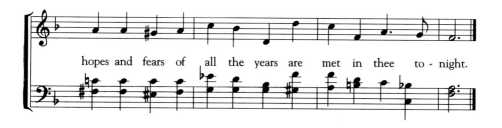

hopes and fears of all the years are met in thee to - night.

# Once in Royal David's City

CECIL FRANCES ALEXANDER WROTE THIS HYMN FOR
'LITTLE CHILDREN' IN 1848. IT IS SUNG EVERY YEAR AT THE
START OF THE SERVICE OF NINE LESSONS AND CAROLS AT
KING'S COLLEGE, CAMBRIDGE, ENGLAND.

1. Once in royal David's city
    Stood a lowly cattle shed,
Where a Mother laid her Baby
    In a manger for his bed:
Mary was that Mother mild,
Jesus Christ her little Child.

2. He came down to earth from heaven,
    Who is God and Lord of all,
And his shelter was a stable,
    And his cradle was a stall;
With the poor, and mean, and lowly,
Lived on earth our Saviour holy.

3. And through all his wondrous childhood
    He would honour and obey,
Love, and watch the lowly Maiden,
    In whose gentle arms he lay;
Christian children all must be
Mild, obedient, good as he.

4. For he is our childhood's pattern,
    Day by day like us he grew,
He was little, weak, and helpless,
    Tears and smiles like us he knew;
And he feeleth for our sadness,
And he shareth in our gladness.

5. And our eyes at last shall see him,
    Through his own redeeming love,
For that Child so dear and gentle
    Is our Lord in heaven above;
And he leads his children on
To the place where he is gone.

6. Not in that poor lowly stable,
    With the oxen standing by,
We shall see him; but in heaven,
    Set at God's right hand on high;
When like stars his children crowned
All in white shall wait around.

Once in ro - yal Da - vid's— ci - ty Stood a

low - ly cat - tle— shed, Where a Moth - er laid— her—

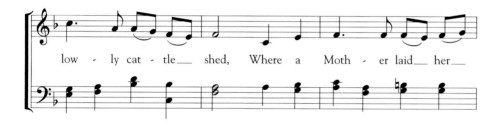

Ba - by In a man - ger for— His— bed: Ma - ry

was that Moth - er mild, Je - sus Christ her lit - tle— Child.

# Patapan

THIS OLD FRENCH CAROL CLEVERLY IMITATES THE SOUND OF
THE FLUTE AND DRUM. THE DIALECT NAME FOR WILLIE IS *GUILLO*.

1. Willie, take your little drum,
   With your whistle, Robin, come!
   When we hear the fife and drum,
      *Tu-re-lu-re-lu, pa-ta-pa-ta-pan;*
   When we hear the flute and drum,
   Christmas should be frolicsome.

2. Thus the men of olden days
   Loved the King of Kings to praise:
   When they hear the fife and drum,
      *Tu-re-lu-re-lu, pa-ta-pa-ta-pan;*
   When they hear the fife and drum,
   Sure our children won't be dumb!

3. God and man are now become
   More at one than fife and drum,
   When you hear the fife and drum,
      *Tu-re-lu-re-lu, pa-ta-pa-ta-pan;*
   When you hear the fife and drum,
   Dance, and make the village hum!

Wil - lie, take your lit - tle drum, With your whis - tle,

Ro - bin, come! When we hear the fife and

drum, Tu - re - lu - re - lu, pa - ta - pa - ta - pan; When we

hear the fife and drum, Christ - mas should be___ fro - lic - some.

# Personent Hodie
## (The Boys' Carol)

THIS STIRRING MELODY COMES FROM THE SAME COLLECTION AS *UNTO US IS BORN A SON* AND WAS GIVEN ITS ENGLISH NAME BY ELIZABETH POSTON, A GREAT COLLECTOR OF CAROLS.

1. Let the boys' cheerful noise
   Sing today none but joys,
   Praise aloud, clear and proud,
   Praise to him in chorus,
   Giv'n from heaven for us,
      Virgin born, born, born,
      Virgin born, born, born,
   Virgin born, on that morn, procreated for us.

2. He who rules heav'n and earth
   Lies in stall at his birth,
   Humble beasts at his feast
   See the Light eternal
   Vanquish realms infernal:
      Satan's done, done, done,
      Satan's done, done, done,
   Satan's done, God has won, victor, he, supernal.

3. Magi come from afar
   See their sun, tiny one,
   Follow far little star,
   At the crib adoring,
   Man to God restoring,
      Gold and myrrh, myrrh, myrrh,
      Gold and myrrh, myrrh, myrrh,
   Gold and myrrh offered there, incense for adoring.

4. Clerk and boy, join in joy,
   Sing as heav'n sings for joy,
   God this day here doth stay,
   Pour we forth the story
   Of his might and glory:
      So to God, God, God,
      So to God, God, God,
   So to God glory be, in the highest, glory.

# Rocking

THIS IS AN OLD CZECHOSLOVAKIAN CAROL.
THE TRANSLATION IS BY PERCY DEARMER.

1. Little Jesus, sweetly sleep, do not stir;
   We will lend a coat of fur,
      We will rock you, rock you, rock you,
      We will rock you, rock you, rock you:
   See the fur to keep you warm,
   Snugly round your tiny form.

2. Mary's little baby, sleep, sweetly sleep,
   Sleep in comfort, slumber deep;
      We will rock you, rock you, rock you,
      We will rock you, rock you, rock you:
   We will serve you all we can,
   Darling, darling little man.

Lit - tle Je - sus, sweet - ly___ sleep, do not___ stir;

We will___ lend a___ coat of___ fur, We will rock you,

rock you, rock you, We will rock you, rock you, rock you: See the fur to

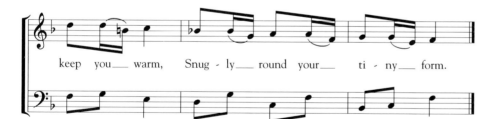

keep you___ warm, Snug - ly___ round your___ ti - ny___ form.

# See Amid the Winter's Snow

EDWARD CASWELL WAS WORKING AMONG THE POOR IN BIRMINGHAM,
ENGLAND, WHEN HE WROTE THE WORDS OF THIS HYMN.

---

1. See amid the winter's snow,
   Born for us on earth below;
   See the tender Lamb appears,
   Promised from eternal years:

   *Hail, thou everblessed morn;*
   *Hail, redemption's happy dawn;*
   *Sing through all Jerusalem,*
   *Christ is born in Bethlehem.*

2. Lo, within a manger lies
   He who built the starry skies;
   He who, throned in height sublime,
   Sits amid the cherubim:

3. Say, ye holy shepherds, say
   What your joyful news to-day;
   Wherefore have ye left your sheep
   On the lonely mountain steep?

4. "As we watched at dead of night,
   Lo, we saw a wondrous light;
   Angels singing 'Peace on earth'
   Told us of the Saviour's birth":

5. Sacred infant, all divine,
   What a tender love was thine,
   Thus to come from highest bliss
   Down to such a world as this:

6. Teach, O teach us, holy Child,
   By thy face so meek and mild,
   Teach us to resemble thee,
   In thy sweet humility:

Ring the joybells - ring!
Christ is born - our King!

See a-mid the win-ter's snow, Born for us on earth be-low;

See the ten-der Lamb ap-pears, Prom-ised from e - ter-nal years:

Hail, thou e - ver bles-sed morn; Hail, re-demp-tion's hap-py dawn;

Sing through all Je - ru - sa-lem, Christ is born in Beth - le - hem.

# Silent Night

THIS CAROL WAS COMPOSED IN AUSTRIA BY JOSEPH MÖHR AND
FRANZ GRÜBER ON CHRISTMAS EVE 1818 AND PERFORMED
THAT EVENING TO GUITAR ACCOMPANIMENT.

1. Silent night, holy night,
   All is calm, all is bright
   Round the Virgin Mother and child,
   Holy infant so tender and mild,
   Sleep in heavenly peace,
   Sleep in heavenly peace.

2. Silent night, holy night,
   Shepherds, hushed, saw the sight,
   Glories stream from heaven afar,
   Heavenly hosts sing Alleluya,
   Christ, the Saviour, is born,
   Christ, the Saviour, is born.

3. Silent night, holy night,
   Son of God, love's pure light
   Radiant beams from thy holy face,
   With the dawn of redeeming grace,
   Jesu, Lord, at thy birth,
   Jesu, Lord, at thy birth.

Si - lent night, ho - ly night, All is calm,

all is bright Round the Vir - gin Moth - er and Child,

Ho - ly in - fant so ten - der and mild, Sleep in heav - en - ly

peace,_____ Sleep in hea - ven - ly peace.

# Sussex Carol

THE FIRST TWO LINES OF THIS TRADITIONAL ENGLISH CAROL
CAN BE REPEATED BY A DIFFERENT GROUP OF SINGERS.

1. On Christmas night all Christians sing,
   To hear the news the angels bring,
   On Christmas night all Christians sing,
   To hear the news the angels bring—
   News of great joy, news of great mirth,
   News of our merciful King's birth.

2. Then why should men on earth be so sad,
   Since our Redeemer made us glad,
   Then why should men on earth be so sad,
   Since our Redeemer made us glad,
   When from our sin he set us free,
   All for to gain our liberty?

3. When sin departs before his grace,
   Then life and health come in its place,
   When sin departs before his grace,
   Then life and health come in its place;
   Angels and men with joy may sing,
   All for to see the newborn King.

4. All out of darkness we have light,
   Which made the Angels sing this night:
   All out of darkness we have light,
   Which made the Angels sing this night:
   "Glory to God and peace to men,
   Now and for evermore. Amen."

On Christ - mas night all Christ - ians sing, To hear the news the

an - gels bring, On Christ - mas night all Christ - ians sing, To hear the news the

an - gels bring — News of great joy, news of great mirth,

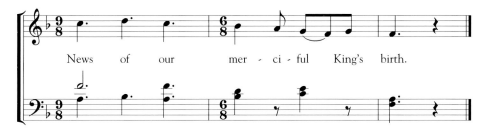

News of our mer - ci - ful King's birth.

# $\mathcal{T}$he Birds Carol
## (from out of a wood did a cuckoo fly)

IN 1921 A CZECH SCHOOLGIRL WAS HEARD SINGING THIS
HAPPY SONG IN THE HILLS OF BOHEMIA AND IT WAS
WRITTEN DOWN FOR THE FIRST TIME.

1. From out of a wood did a cuckoo fly,
    Cuckoo,
  He came to a manger with joyful cry,
    Cuckoo,
  He hopped, he curtsied, round he flew,
  And loud his jubilation grew,
    Cuckoo, cuckoo, cuckoo.

2. A pigeon flew over to Galilee,
    Vrercroo,
  He strutted, and cooed, and was full of glee,
    Vrercroo,
  And showed with jewelled wings unfurled,
  His joy that Christ was in the world,
    Vrercroo, vrercroo, vrercroo.

3. A dove settled down upon Nazareth,
    Tsucroo,
  And tenderly chanted with all his breath,
    Tsucroo,
  "O you," he cooed, "so good and true,
  My beauty do I give to you—
    Tsucroo, tsucroo, tsucroo."

From out of a wood did a cuck - oo fly, Cuck -

-oo, He came to a man - ger with joy - ful

cry, Cuck - oo, He hopped, he curt - sied,

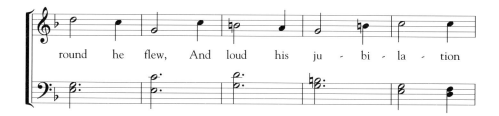

round he flew, And loud his ju - bi - la - tion

grew, Cuck - oo, cuck - oo, cuck - oo.

# The First Nowell

*NOWELL* IS A WORD UNIQUE TO CHRISTMAS AND IS AN EXPRESSION OF JOY AT THIS TIME. THE NAME *NOËL* IS OFTEN GIVEN TO CHILDREN BORN ON CHRISTMAS DAY.

1. The first Nowell the Angel did say
   Was to certain poor shepherds in fields as they lay;
   In fields where they lay keeping their sheep,
   On a cold winter's night that was so deep:

   *Nowell, Nowell, Nowell, Nowell,*
   *Born is the King of Israel.*

2. They looked up and saw a star,
   Shining in the east, beyond them far;
   And to the earth it gave great light,
   And it continued both day and night:

3. And by the light of that same star,
   Three Wise Men came from country far;
   To seek for a king was their intent,
   And to follow the star wherever it went:

4. This star drew nigh to the north-west;
   O'er Bethlehem it took its rest,
   And there it did both stop and stay
   Right over the place where Jesus lay:

5. Then entered in those Wise Men three,
   Full rev'rently upon their knee,
   And offered there in his presence
   Their gold and myrrh and frankincense:

6. Then let us all with one accord
   Sing praises to our heav'nly Lord,
   That hath made heav'n and earth of nought,
   And with his blood mankind hath bought:

The first Nowell the Angel did say Was to certain poor shepherds in fields as they lay; In fields where they lay keeping their sheep, On a cold winter's night that was so deep: Nowell, Nowell, Nowell, Nowell, Born is the King of Israel.

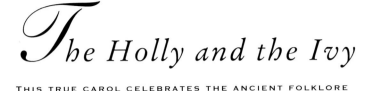

# The Holly and the Ivy

THIS TRUE CAROL CELEBRATES THE ANCIENT FOLKLORE
ASSOCIATED WITH HOLLY AND IVY. SOME PEOPLE STILL
CONSIDER IT UNLUCKY TO BRING IVY INDOORS.

1. The holly and the ivy, when they are both full grown,
   Of all the trees that are in the wood, the holly bears the crown:

   *O, the rising of the sun and the running of the deer,*
   *The playing of the merry organ, sweet singing in the choir.*

2. The holly bears a blossom, as white as the lily flower,
   And Mary bore sweet Jesus Christ to be our sweet Saviour:

3. The holly bears a berry, as red as any blood,
   And Mary bore sweet Jesus Christ to do poor sinners good:

4. The holly bears a prickle, as sharp as any thorn,
   And Mary bore sweet Jesus Christ on Christmas Day in the morn:

5. The holly bears a bark, as bitter as any gall,
   And Mary bore sweet Jesus Christ for to redeem us all:

6. The holly and the ivy, when they are both full grown,
   Of all the trees that are in the wood, the holly bears the crown.

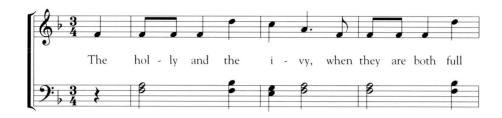

The hol - ly and the i - vy, when they are both full

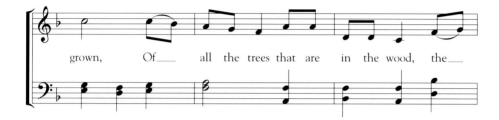

grown, Of___ all the trees that are in the wood, the___

hol - ly bears the crown: O, the ri - sing of the

sun ___ and the run - ning of the deer, The ___

*play - ing of the mer - ry or - gan, sweet ___ sing - ing in the choir.*

# The Twelve Days of Christmas

THIS TRADITIONAL ENGLISH CAROL RETAINS ITS IMMENSE
APPEAL AND IS ONE OF THE FEW CAROLS TO CELEBRATE
THE GIVING OF CHRISTMAS PRESENTS ON A SCALE
TO PUT US ALL TO SHAME.

————

1. On the first day of Christmas my true love sent to me
   A partridge in a pear tree.

2. On the second day of Christmas my true love sent to me
   Two turtle doves
   And a partridge in a pear tree.

3. On the third day of Christmas my true love sent to me
   Three French hens,
   Two turtle doves
   And a partridge in a pear tree.

4. On the fourth day of Christmas my true love sent to me
   Four calling birds, etc.

5. On the fifth day of Christmas my true love sent to me
   Five gold rings, etc.

6. On the sixth day of Christmas my true love sent to me
   Six geese a-laying, etc.

7. On the seventh day of Christmas my true love sent to me
   Seven swans a-swimming, etc.

8. On the eighth day of Christmas my true love sent to me
   Eight maids a-milking, etc.

9. On the ninth day of Christmas my true love sent to me
   Nine ladies dancing, etc.

10. On the tenth day of Christmas my true love sent to me
    Ten lords a-leaping, etc.

11. On the eleventh day of Christmas my true love sent to me
    Eleven pipers piping, etc.

12. On the twelfth day of Christmas my true love sent to me
    Twelve drummers drumming, etc.

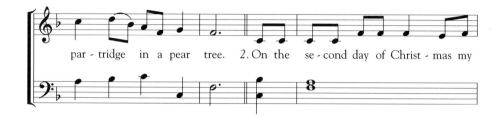

1. On the first day of Christ - mas my true love sent to me A

par - tridge in a pear tree. 2. On the se - cond day of Christ - mas my

true love sent to me Two tur - tle doves And a par - tridge in a pear tree.

3. On the third day of Christ - mas my true love sent to me

Three French hens, Two tur - tle doves And a par - tridge in a pear tree.

par - tridge in a pear tree. 6. On the sixth day of Christ - mas my

true love sent to me Six geese a - lay - ing, Five gold

rings, Four call - ing birds, Three French hens, Two tur - tle doves And a

**Fine**

par - tridge ——— in a pear tree. 7.–12. On the

*Repeat as necessary*

seventh day of Christ - mas my true love sent to me seven swans a - swim - ming
eighth                                                eight maids a - milk - ing
ninth                                                 nine    la - dies dan - cing
tenth                                                 ten    lords a - leap - ing
eleventh                                              eleven pi - pers pi - ping
twelfth                                               twelve drum - mers drum - ming

*Continue from ✛ to Fine*

# Tomorrow Shall Be My Dancing Day

THE WORD 'CAROL' ORIGINALLY MEANT 'TO DANCE'
SO THIS IS A VERY AUTHENTIC CAROL. 'SILLY' IN THE
THIRD VERSE MEANS 'SIMPLE'.

———

1. Tomorrow shall be my dancing day:
     I would my true love did so chance
   To see the legend of my play,
     To call my true love to my dance:

   *Sing O my love, O my love, my love, my love;*
   *This have I done for my true love.*

2. Then was I born of a virgin pure,
     Of her I took fleshly substance;
   Thus was I knit to man's nature;
     To call my true love to my dance:

3. In a manger laid and wrapped I was,
     So very poor, this was my chance,
   Betwixt an ox and a silly poor ass,
     To call my true love to my dance:

To - mor - row shall be___ my danc - ing day: I

would my true love did so chance To see the le - gend

of___ my play, To call my true___ love to___ my dance:

Sing O my___ love, O___ my love, my love, my

love; This have I done___ for my___ true love.

# Unto Us is Born a Son

THIS ROUSING CAROL WAS SUNG IN LATIN IN FIFTEENTH-
CENTURY GERMANY. THE MELODY ECHOES THE RINGING
OF BELLS AND THE PLAYING OF ORGANS.

1. Unto us is born a Son,
    King of choirs supernal:
   See on earth his life begun,
    Of lords the Lord eternal,
    Of lords the Lord eternal.

2. Christ, from heav'n descending low,
    Comes on earth a stranger;
   Ox and ass their owner know,
    Be-cradled in the manger,
    Be-cradled in the manger.

3. This did Herod sore affray,
    And grievously bewilder,
   So he gave the word to slay,
    And slew the little childer,
    And slew the little childer.

4. Of his love and mercy mild
    This the Christmas story;
   O that Mary's gentle Child
    Might lead us up to Glory,
    Might lead us up to Glory.

84

Un - to us is born a Son, King of choirs su -

-per - nal: See on earth his life be - gun, Of

lords the Lord e - ter - nal, of lords the Lord e - ter - nal.

# Wassail Song

Wassailing, or roving the streets in groups seeking refreshment at every door, must have been great fun for the wassailers if not for everybody else.

1. Here we come a-wassailing
    Among the leaves so green,
   Here we come a-wandering
    So fair to be seen.

   *Love and joy come to you,*
   *And to you your wassail too,*
    *And God bless you and send you a*
    *happy New Year,*
    *And God send you a happy New Year.*

2. Our wassail cup is made
    Of the rosemary tree,
   And so is your beer
    Of the best barley.

3. We are not daily beggars
    That beg from door to door,
   But we are neighbours' children
    Whom you have seen before.

4. Good Master and good Mistress,
    As you sit by the fire,
   Pray for us poor children
    Who're wand'ring in the mire.

5. We have got a little purse
    Of stretching leather skin;
   Give some of your small change
    To line it well within.

6. Call the butler of this house,
    Put on his golden ring;
   Let him bring us pots of beer:
    The better we shall sing.

7. Bring us out a table
    And spread it with a cloth;
   Bring us out a mouldy cheese,
    And some of your Christmas loaf.

8. God bless the Master of this house,
    Likewise the Mistress too;
   And all the little children
    That round the table go.

9. And all your kin and kinsfolk
    That dwell both far and near;
   I wish you Merry Christmas,
    And happy New Year.

The Wassail Bowl.

Here we come a - was - sail - ing A - mong the leaves so

green,_____ Here we come a - wan - der - ing So

fair__ to be seen. Love and joy come to you, And to

you your was - sail too, And God bless you and send__ you a

hap - py New Year, And God send you a hap - py New Year.

# *We Three Kings of Orient are*

JOHN HENRY HOPKINS JR. WROTE THE WORDS AND MUSIC
FOR THIS CAROL IN WILLIAMSPORT, PENNSYLVANIA IN 1857.
IT CAN BE PERFORMED DRAMATICALLY.

1. We three kings of Orient are;
   Bearing gifts we traverse afar;
   Field and fountain, moor and mountain,
   Following yonder star:

   *O star of wonder, star of night,*
   *Star with Royal beauty bright,*
   *Westward leading, still proceeding,*
   *Guide us to thy perfect light.*

Melchior:
2. Born a king on Bethlehem plain,
   Gold I bring, to crown him again—
   King for ever, ceasing never,
   Over us all to reign:

Caspar:
3. Frankincense to offer have I;
   Incense owns a deity nigh:
   Prayer and praising, all men raising,
   Worship him, God most high:

Balthazar:
4. Myrrh is mine; its bitter perfume
   Breathes a life of gathering gloom;
   Sorrowing, sighing, bleeding, dying,
   Sealed in the stone-cold tomb:

5. Glorious now, behold him arise,
   King, and God, and sacrifice!
   Heav'n sings alleluya,
   Alleluya the earth replies:

# We Wish You a Merry Christmas

THIS FAVOURITE WITH CAROL SINGERS IS A TRADITIONAL
WASSAIL SONG FROM THE WEST OF ENGLAND.

1. We wish you a merry Christmas,
   We wish you a merry Christmas,
   We wish you a merry Christmas
   And a happy New Year.

   *Good tidings we bring*
   *To you and your kin;*
   *We wish you a merry Christmas*
   *And a happy New Year.*

2. Now bring us some figgy pudding,
   Now bring us some figgy pudding,
   Now bring us some figgy pudding
   And bring some out here.

3. For we all like figgy pudding,
   We all like figgy pudding,
   We all like figgy pudding,
   So bring some out here.

4. And we won't go till we've got some,
   We won't go till we've got some,
   We won't go till we've got some,
   So bring some out here.

Ring the joybells – ring!
Christ is born – our King!

90

# While Shepherds Watched

NAHUM TATE BASED HIS HYMN ON THE GOSPEL OF SAINT LUKE.
THE TUNE IS AN OLD ENGLISH PSALM TUNE.

1. While shepherds watched their flocks by night,
    All seated on the ground,
   The Angel of the Lord came down,
    And glory shone around.

2. "Fear not" said he (for mighty dread
    Had seized their troubled mind);
   "Glad tidings of great joy I bring
    To you and all mankind.

3. "To you in David's town this day
    Is born of David's line
   A Saviour, who is Christ the Lord;
    And this shall be the sign:

4. "The heav'nly Babe you there shall find
    To human view displayed,
   All meanly wrapped in swathing bands,
    And in a manger laid."

5. Thus spake the Seraph; and forthwith
    Appeared a shining throng
   Of Angels praising God, who thus
    Addressed their joyful song:

6. "All glory be to God on high,
    And on the earth be peace;
   Goodwill henceforth from heav'n to men
    Begin and never cease."

While shep - herds watched their flocks by night, All

sea - ted on the ground, The An - gel of the

Lord came down, And glo - ry shone a - round.

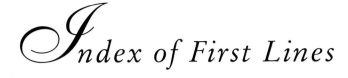

# Index of First Lines

# Picture Acknowledgements

The illustrations in this book are courtesy of:
The Bridgeman Art Library
The Mary Evans Picture Library
Fine Art Photographs